HOW TO GET HER TO SAY YES TO A DATE

Copyright

2022 © Gary Maxwell

All rights reserved.

ISBN:

TABLE OF CONTENTS

FOREWORD

The art of asking girls will be much easier if you study over time. It does not mean trying everything. You are very happy to share your ideas for friends and colleagues. All women are very different, and you have to spend time to know, not only their tastes and aversions, but also their personality. Time is needed to find out, especially when reserved or very personal. This book provides practical advice. You can meet her and persuade her to go out with her. It's not a simple solution. If you want to succeed, you need to be ready to spend time and effort.

This is a step -by -step process, and you can understand how the spirit of a woman works, and be able to communicate normally with the potential date. Your approach must be adapted according to the girl's personality. If she goes out of her and is easy to access, she can go ahead and ask her to leave. But if she is shy and reserved, she can more think about her approach or may be afraid. This electronic book will present you a secret that helps you improve your chances of succeeding when you want an appointment changes in action and society have facilitated the creation of relationships for people. It is not uncommon for the relationship to start with a problem, several or days from the first

meeting. However, in some cases, more communication and

persuasion may require accepting the date of the girls. This is an

opportunity to improve.

CHAPTER ONE

Understanding the Feminine Gender

I'll describe the types of girls you might encounter in this chapter. I'll also suggest some ways for you to get to know them better.

1. Girls With Calm Attitudes

You should look for this kind of woman if you want to settle down with someone for the long term or perhaps your entire life. She will tackle everything with a serious mindset. Because she is a "one-man woman," she will anticipate that in a relationship, the man will hold the power. She's probably going to be obedient and eager to please. She does, however, have unalterable standards and routines that are nearly impossible to alter. She will judge you according to her standards and anticipates that you share her aspirations for the future.

2. Girls Who Strike Out

These gals seem to be tranquil girls, yet they are completely different from them. However, they are deeply serious about a romantic connection, and they will look to you for commitment in return. These women relish flirting. They prefer it when you focus your attention on them. They are friendly and entertaining to be around, yet they hate routine and monotony.

3. Girls Who Don't Look As Good

Even though these females may not be the prettiest, they are friendly and highly supportive. Instead of merely being a date, they could very possibly become your lifelong closest friend. They tend to be quite apprehensive of boys who are attracted to them since they feel they have nothing to give in the appeal stakes. They are suspicious of the motives of boys who make sentimental gestures and offer flowery comments. They are independent thinkers who anticipate that boys will be more drawn to them for their intellect than their beauty. In terms of relational importance, they place friendship significantly higher than love. You might have to follow suit and give up on romantic gestures and dates.

4. The Boring Girls

It's common to encounter girls who are uninteresting. That typically indicates that you lack common ground upon which to base a relationship.

When you first meet, the female could come across as vivacious and fun. But after you've covered all the getting to know you stuff. You'll probably run out of topics to discuss. Your lack of common hobbies or interests will cause your relationship to fall apart rapidly. It could be preferable not to begin.

CHAPTER TWO

Strategic Planning to Ask Her Out

When you're planning to ask a girl out, there are a few things you need to plan. You will be led through the planning in this chapter.

Throughout your life, it's likely that you may encounter some challenging circumstances. But asking a girl out on a date and getting it right might be one of the hardest. You're expecting she'll answer right away with "yes." However, you could not always be so fortunate and she might refuse or make reasons why she is unable to date you. Here are some suggestions on how to persuade the woman to accept your invitation on a date.

1. Slim your chance of Failure

The likelihood that the female you are asking out will reject you increases if you are a complete stranger to her. She may not even be aware that you are "Jack the Ripper." Her response will probably be a self-preservation maneuver with little regard for you. She will put into practice what she has been told since she was young, "not to talk to, or go with strangers." A rejection shouldn't make you feel less confident. You must be patient and spend some time getting to know one another each other more thoroughly. It would be lot simpler for you to ask the girl out on a date if you can get her to hang out with you and your buddies. If She has seen overtime that you can be a fun guy, therefore she is more likely to say yes.

2. Be impulsive and don't be scared to display your compassionate side.

Show her that you are intelligent and that you are able to discuss subjects other than what is happening at home or at school. Take the time to learn about her interests and likes by talking about topics or activities that really fascinate you. Everything revolves around open, natural communication and getting to know one another.

3. Prepare Your Date's Logistics in Advance

You might also try charm and delicate persuasion if she says she already has arrangements for the evening you want to take her out. She may alter her plans if she senses that you are a good time to be around and that you appeal to her. Or you might ask her which night she would be comfortable with.

4.   **Be ready to do the asking**

Keep away from the false hope that a female may ask you out on a date. Contrary to popular opinion, relatively few girls will approach you and ask you out. Be ready to be the one to ask for a chance if you don't want to miss out.

5.   **Selecting the Appropriate Time**

It's crucial to make sure the time you ask a girl out is appropriate. When you quickly approach her and inquire, she won't accept until she's had a chance to get to know you. It Several friend gatherings could be necessary before you locate the ideal time. You must exercise patience and trust your gut and become adept at interpreting the cues she is providing you should have a natural sense of when to advance to dating.

6.   **Knowing When to Approach Her for a Date**

There are a number of indicators that the girl is ready to take you out on a date. Additionally to the manner she looks your way. Even if you chat about uninteresting topics or don't say much, she will still be interested in you. You must rely on your intuition and innate capacity to discern when it's time to ask her out on a date.

CHAPTER THREE

Romantic Tips to Deploy

You should approach a girl with style and romanticism if you want to ask her out on a date. The suggestions in this chapter will assist you in developing your amorous side, your character.

Having a female as a friend is one thing; the challenging part can be advancing to a romantic connection. If you approach it, making a smooth transition will be simple in the proper manner. What you say and how you act both, asking a lady out could be the difference between success and failure.

1. Don't be afraid to display your caring or feminine side

You must let a girl know if you are interested in her know. Often, this entails lowering your 'macho' attitude, conduct, and letting her realize that you're more kind and a kindlier disposition. If you appear to have too much testosterone could scare or otherwise affect the girl she will find reasons not to go out with you. The majority of men are unwilling to acknowledge that especially when speaking to other people, they have a feminine aspect. However, the most effective method to persuade the woman to go on a showing her that you are compassionate and understanding on a date nature. If you do this and she keeps turning you, maybe you should let her go and look for another girl to enquire about a date.

2. Have faith in yourself

Although you might not be the most appealing man on the globe, you might not be the ugliest. You must have strength in the conviction that you can offer a girl something. However, finding the ideal balance between being self- confident, if you want to be, either being arrogant or confident successfully drew the girl in. You might be surprised if, like the majority of men starting out in the dating world, you believe you lack any romantic qualities. Taking a few quick actions can bring out the romantic in you.

3. Take a seat and make a list

You can make a list of the things you need to remember if you have trouble recalling things. If you, girls will be quite impressed when you commemorate their birthday or other noteworthy events without needing to be reminded, anniversaries. The you should at the very least send her a card, but you will sending flowers will earn you a lot more points, To celebrate, give her chocolates or take her out to a nice supper. Additionally, you can utilize your list to record her loves and dislikes like what is her least favorite color, what is her favorite color, etc? It will help you save a ton of money, grief if you select a gift that she really likes as gift for the awesome occasion

4. Make the first move

It might be challenging to determine when your relationship with a girl is ready to advance to the next level. As will many girls be hesitant to take action; it is up to you to decide, the initial action. If you go above the call by acting too if you become overly passionate too soon, the relationship may end. You must begin by bidding farewell with a wave or a little kiss on the cheek. When holding hands, you can while strolling or watching a movie in a chair, the more you acquire knowing her will make it simpler for you to read the signs. When she's ready to take the relationship further, she will let you know.

5. Communication

Any partnership needs to have open communication. It is a fantastic tool that offers the a chance for the couple to learn more about one another one more tick The discussions ought to be casual and should be designed so that they can study and listen just as much as involve speaking. The girl may at first seem timid or hesitant to discuss herself or her interests

She'll unwind if you talk about common interests or pastimes. Asking her questions may help you get a response from her. However, make sure not to give her the impression that she is being questioned by you.

6. Whenever she needs you, be there for her.

You need to show your compassionate side and be there for your girl if she's upset for any reason or just feels under the weather. There may be no treatment for a physical condition, but you may offer moral support only by showing up and paying attention demonstrates your genuine concern that might assist in enhancing her emotional state.

7. Verify That She Notices You

Since the girl doesn't even know you, there is little point in wasting your time and effort on a show for her are present. You must ensure that your actions include, identify a cause that appeals to her and invite her to participate or to express her viewpoint to you about what you want to do. For some people, unfortunately, that does mean you need to speak before attempting to impress her, get to know her.

CHAPTER FOUR

How to Enhance Getting a Yes

Read the advice in this chapter if you are asking girls out and getting turned down to figure out what you are doing incorrectly.

Nowadays, society views dating practices considerably more casually than it did when our parents and grandparents were young. It was hardly ever done for people to be in many partnerships at once same moment. Dating was serious business, particularly when a longer-term relationship is often over by marriage. In contrast, it is not uncommon for people to regularly switch dating partners, have multiple relationships at the same moment. People are far less likely to enter this place with their first date, into a marriage. Unfortunately, the current trend of experimenting with numerous dates might be beneficial while looking for the appropriate companion, terrible outcomes of a criminal character.

1. Being prepared and on time is essential.

Getting ready for a first date is crucial. You must begin by taking into account if you want to generate a favorable impression, way you'll appear. Think about what you and your date might do. How do you show yourself, in your opinion? Could she do it? See that you have tried your best? Putting forth an attempt to your appearance, particularly on the first date, will contribute to make a good first impression. On your first date, being on time is equally as crucial as being polite; appearance the message despite being a few minutes late sending the wrong signals before your date even begins. You are better off scheduling a few minutes early for your meeting hours early.

2. Remaining positive and calm

On a first date, try to control your nerves and maintain your composure. Take a few deep breaths if you are feeling a bit stressed out. Before your date arrives, taking a few breaths can help you relax.

If you are susceptible to becoming upset by low quality next you must choose the location for your date using the service cautiously. If you lose, you won't get any bonus points about the little thing, lose your anger, or start a fight. Keeping your composure if you have a case to make it expressing dissatisfaction makes a positive impression and displays that you possess good judgment.

3. Don't be afraid to compliment her.

Anyone who claims they don't value compliments, particularly women, is lying. Though, the sincere compliments are necessary to avoid offending your date seize on it. Despite the fact that there are moments when you might have to use your diplomacy and sensitivity, especially if she inquires about your opinion on her new dress you were unaware of a new hairdo or outfit. If you tell her you detest it, she won't thank you for being honest.

It demonstrates your respect and regard for your date when you pay attention to what she has to say and respect her right to her own viewpoints. IF YOU PERMIT your focus to wander or interrupt you frequently in order to impose her opinions above your own, you probably won't get a second outing. It is your obligation to maintain as much of a natural flow in the dialogue as you can. Making sure there aren't any significant gaps in the discussion. Keeping a running record of the subjects you can mention someone you know will contribute to the discussion engaging your date helps you avoid awkward situations silences.

4. Trust Your Gut Feelings and Tell the Truth

You probably won't get around to sharing your date all of your darkest secrets on the first date. There are some things, though, for which you must be awake. When they are in front of you, you will instantly recognize them if you want the connection to endure and grow. You need to let her know after the initial date. She can do so she must decide if she wants to keep dating you. You should consider carefully what might occur if she learned prior to getting information about your secret from another source before telling her. If you don't inform her, it will be more difficult if she finds out in the long run.

However, if she inquires directly, you can always tell lies. If you do, you might feel bad about lying, and when the truth eventually comes out, you'll have to deal with the consequences to justify your deception. That may be sufficient to complete your relationship.

5. Stay upbeat through negative experiences

If you can get through life without encountering a difficult moment you will be incredibly lucky if you experience rejection in the dating game.

Almost everyone will know at least one poor person, if not more at least once in their lives, people date. Simply take what you can from it, and then go on. You must acknowledge that life is not always a "bed of roses" and it's all your fault it didn't work out. If you feel that you even slightly contributed to the breakdown of the date, you may then take precautions to make sure that none of your future dates will be ruined by the same issues. You must have optimism about finding the ideal date in the future for you.

6. Dedicated to Possibly Finding a Lifetime Partner

If you are dedicated to finding a companion for life, if you want to date a female casually, you need be explicit about your own thoughts around what you're seeking. As well you must be honest with the girl because she could not feel the similar to how you feel about a lifetime partnership. There are some women who would be prepared to a lifetime commitment to a spouse for a variety of reasons but unless you've spent some time getting to know each other. Other first typically refers to dating. There is none promises that you will get along or that a lifetime relationship will endure.

7. Successful dating experiences

It can be a terrifying prospect if you're new to dating or coming back after a long absence. You should review your skills and expertise if you wish to locate a suitable dating companion. Talk to friends and other people who may have recently gone on a date or are going through the same thing while people-watching to see how others are behaving or hear them share their experiences. They will undoubtedly be a reliable source of guidance and advice on how to approach it.

CHAPTER 5

Five Guidelines for Approaching a Girl

I'm going to outline the five guiding principles for asking a girl

out in this chapter.

Choosing the appropriate course of action can be quite nerve-

wracking. You need to take a few factors into account, but

these are the five guidelines you need to follow at all times.

1. Do not call her right away.

Once you obtain the girl's phone number, resist the urge to call

her right away. If you seem overly eager, she can feel that

you're putting pressure on her and become annoyed, your entire

group. Allow her enough time to adjust to the notion that you

will be make a call to her, but don't wait too long because

someone else might, may succeed before you. In most cases,

awaiting twenty-four to best is forty-eight hours.

2. Do not approach her with a date request right away.

Don't just leap into a call when you do get around to making

one requesting a date with her. Spend some time discussing

either the overall state of things or a shared interest. When your

gut is telling you, make plans to meet for coffee or lunch as friends if you feel that you two need to get to know one another a little better before going on a date. Instead, if you are planning any kind of social gathering you both say that she is welcome to go along with you. That in this manner, you are not really asking her out on a date, but it gives if she does, it gives you the chance to get to know her better.

3. Put more fun than stress into your date.

Some individuals can make their debut such a big deal, they overlook having fun on dates your daughter will become much more impressed If you are at ease and can convey to her that you are having fun with her and whatever it is that you are doing, she will be impressed.

If you are worried about making the date a success, if you're pushing too hard for success, you probably are, and that is unprofessional and can be just as damaging as being blasé and overconfident in the circumstance. When picking a location or activity for your first date, be consistent to what you are accustomed to. You'll possess enough anxiety to deal with, but not enough to the anxiety that results from adjusting to a new concurrently with another setting or activity.

4. Tell her your plans

It is quite simple to make the wrong decision when deciding what to do and where to go on a first date, so just tell her your plans instead of asking her. There must be a taker the initiative, and you ought to do it. Think up some concepts tell your date what you have in mind, but keep in mind you're considering assuming she doesn't protest or propose different ideas, you should go ahead and organize the plans.

If your girl does not agree with your proposals, ask her what she prefers to do in its place. You two could to achieve what you both want, you must make a compromise.

Depending on how well you know each other besides, it will increase your chances of setting up dates that she'll find appealing. You'll soon find out if she's willing to allow you to forward with plans for without asking her first, your dates.

These days, many females demand an equal voice in decisions and if they don't understand, they might think you're being rude, dominating and hegemonic. Alternatively, there a few gals nearby who are content to escape all the decisions leaving you, be the judge.

5. Persuade Your Girl

You have the chance to gather information on your first date information about your girl, then assess your likelihood of be compatible if you decide to date again, exactly how she is

You must examine yourself and create an opinion about her personality. If you find out that you both are arguing over trivial matters, you may have big disagreements when it comes to making important life decisions. Compromise might not be an option, alternative until both parties agree.

CHAPTER 6

What Not to Do When You Ask a Girl Out

When you ask a girl out, there are a few typical blunders that you should avoid. In this chapter, I'll explain.

Often, knowing how to impress a female is insufficient. If you want to succeed, you must be aware of the dangers and how you may avoid them. You can learn more in this chapter about the traps to watch out for.

1. Negative Thoughts

Whether you allow yourself to think bad thoughts consciously or unconsciously, they will manifest in your body language. If your date has the intelligence to understand your body language or discerns your unfavorable attitude from your just the chat will turn your date off.

In other circumstances, it may also keep you from asking women out. Only you are capable of eliminating that negativity. You must focus on what you already have your best qualities and get rid of the bad ideas to boost your self-assurance.

2. Keep your distance from a girl who isn't interested in you

Pushing for a date after the girl has already declined is one of the biggest blunders you can make. If you keep pushing her even when it clearly noticeable from all indication she isn't interested in you. That might become a significant issue and land you in serious danger.

You must believe what she says without question, and if she back off if she declines your invitation for a date. You must pivot shift your focus somewhere else.

You must be observant to determine the girl's level of interest But if she is simply trying to be difficult by refusing when you first ask invite her out. If she begins to ignore you, you can be quite certain that she meant no when she said she tries to avoid your company. If she doesn't make an effort to avoid you or persists it might be worth waiting a while and trying to talk to you again.

3. Control your jealousy and insecurity

A further, frequently unforgivable error is to let jealousy and insecurity creep into your partnership. If you begin acting in when she interacts with other men, moody, or you complain you are on a rant over her hanging out with her girlfriends sliding scale. Usually, once it starts, it only gets worse. Keep telling yourself that your girl is beautiful all the time. She is with you even though she is not in your possession as desires to be.

4. Fear of Being Rejected

Being rejected by a female might damage your self-esteem and your ego. Usually, you already have a lot of thoughts if it's just your ego and you'll persuade yourself that it was she and no actual harm was done to you. However, if your self-confidence really suffers, you might find it more difficult to have the bravery to ask a different female out. You can always discuss it with a trustworthy individual who can assist you in realizing that it is not the end of the globe and assist you as you continue your journey. It will be more difficult the longer you wait for it to progress.

CHAPTER 7

First impression Lasts a Lifetime

If you're trying to impress a female quickly, you're in the wrong place a waste of time. They might be drawn to you, but likely to take some work on your part before falling at your feet. First impressions do matter, though, so if you make bad first impression, you'll have to work much harder to alter it.

1. Pay attention to your body language

Be conscious of yourself and what your body language conveys about you. A female may provide a lot of information about you based on your body language, before you approach or speak to her, seeing others while considering their physical characteristics language is telling you, it might make you more conscious of how you appear.

2. Keep some of your personality's secrets hidden and reveal Slowly

It takes time to get to know someone, and we all have a tendency to till we get to know the person better, we should act appropriately. That is acceptable unless you are concealing a dark, secretive side to your character.

It is simple to provide the justification that you didn't want to scare her off on the first date, but if she learns you weren't being completely honest with her, she can feel even more betrayed from the beginning.

3. Be in charge of your date.

You can anticipate having some since you asked the girl out, control over your activities and whereabouts. The girl could be content to watch from a distance as you grab the reins, but you don't assume that at your peril.

Keep in mind that you and I are on an equal footing. You two are each entitled to your own opinions. the initial date especially as you learn more about one another there shouldn't be any justification for arguments, whether they are civil or not. As you learn more, steer the discourse away from potentially contentious topics more info regarding one another

4. Have fun and be amusing.

If the two of you have taken the time to get to know one another, then prior to going on a date, you'll probably discover it's a lot of work. It's simpler to be yourself around others and you can just unwind and enjoy yourself.

If the date is blind or you haven't gotten a chance to meet each other, you'll probably be more tense. Not at all the ideal moment to check out a brand-new restaurant or venue never visited before. It will be simpler to focus on each other and unwind the more accustomed you both are to the surroundings.

Conclusion

It takes tact and expertise to ask a girl out, which you'll develop with experience. You should experience some good and some negative encounters. You must take note of the excellent ones and leave the negative ones in the past so you can go on.

Never allow a negative event to diminish you since that is the secret to obtaining your next. Girls prefer to date men that exude confidence and assurance perpetually.

Not all women only want what they can obtain from a relationship. However, if you do see one who is extremely materialistic and want to date her, you'll need to deep pockets to maintain the connection. Until you run out of cash, you might discover when she finds someone who can give her more, she may leave you fast or she may be difficult to break up with. This e-book was created to provide you an understanding of information on how to increase your chances of getting dates. Unfortunately, since each person is unique and you rarely do two people instantly click together. You do need to develop a relationship with each other's personalities prior to her potentially going out, some background information on the girl and you.

Additionally, have a mastery into the mentality and personality of women, but as you have probably heard a lot of times, "who can understand a woman's mind"? The response is most likely not you, but trying can be enjoyable. So why not enjoy yourself? Best of Luck